6

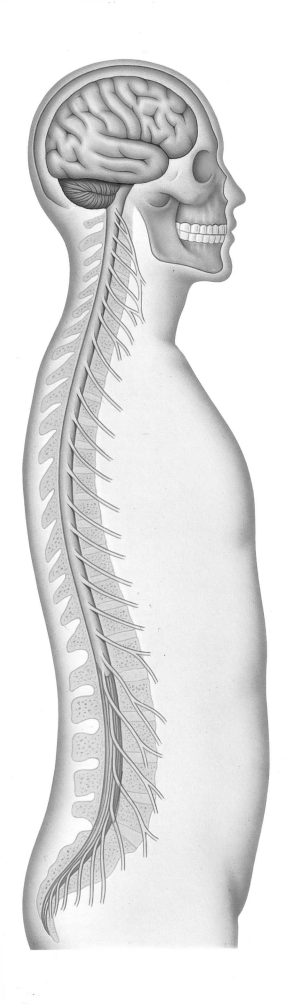

The Brain and Nervous System

Steve Parker

RSVP

RAINTREE
STECK-VAUGHN
PUBLISHERS

The Steck-Vaughn Company

Austin, Texas

TITLES IN THE SERIES

The Heart and Circulatory System
The Stomach and Digestive System
The Brain and Nervous System
The Lungs and Respiratory System
The Skeleton and Muscular System
The Reproductive System

Published by Raintree Steck-Vaughn Publishers,
an imprint of Steck-Vaughn Company

Library of Congress Cataloging-in-Publication Data
Parker, Steve.
The brain and nervous system / Steve Parker.
p.   cm.—(The human body)
Includes bibliographical references and index.
Summary: Examines the different parts and functions of the brain and nervous system.
ISBN 0-8172-4802-1
1. Brain—Juvenile literature.
2. Nervous system—Juvenile literature.
[1. Brain. 2. Nervous system.]
I. Title. II. Series: Parker, Steve. Human body.
QP361.5.P35   1997
612.8'2—dc21   96-36804

Printed in Italy. Bound in the United States.
1 2 3 4 5 6 7 8 9 0 01 00 99 98 97

Picture Acknowledgments
The publishers would like to thank the following for use of their photographs:
Popperfoto 4, 38; Science Photo Library 12, 31, 34, 35, 40, 42, 44;
The remaining pictures are from the Wayland Picture Library.

CONTENTS

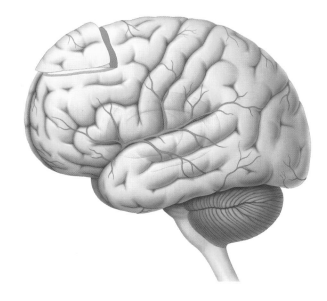

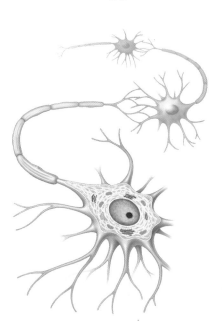

Introduction

Imagine a huge school, without the principal and school office to control and coordinate all of its activities. The teachers would not know which classrooms to use, or which subjects they should teach. No one would buy new books, computers, and equipment. Without a timetable, the students could go where they wanted, when they wanted. There would be no tests, exams, or homework. It might sound like fun, but no one would learn anything.

The body has its own "principal" and "office" too. They are the brain and **nerves**. The brain is in overall control of all body processes. The nerves send messages out to parts of the body and receive messages from them, to make sure all body activities are organized and coordinated. This happens every second, of every day—thoughout life.

Your brain is where you have thoughts, ideas, and emotions, where you concentrate, daydream, learn, and remember. These are called conscious processes. You are aware of them as they happen. Yet even while your body sleeps, your brain is busy. It automatically controls body processes that are not in your conscious awareness, like breathing, heartbeat, and digestion of food.

The brain and nerves are sometimes compared with a computer in charge of an electronic network of machines and devices. But as this book shows, the brain is more complex and wonderful than any computer.

▼ Since the beginning of time, people have wondered about the links between the brain, the mind, the soul and thoughts and emotions. Aristotle (384–322 B.C.), of Ancient Greece, believed that the body's center for thoughts and emotions was not the brain, but the heart. French scientist and thinker René Descartes (1596–1650) suggested that the mind and soul were somehow outside the body, linked to the brain through the eyes.

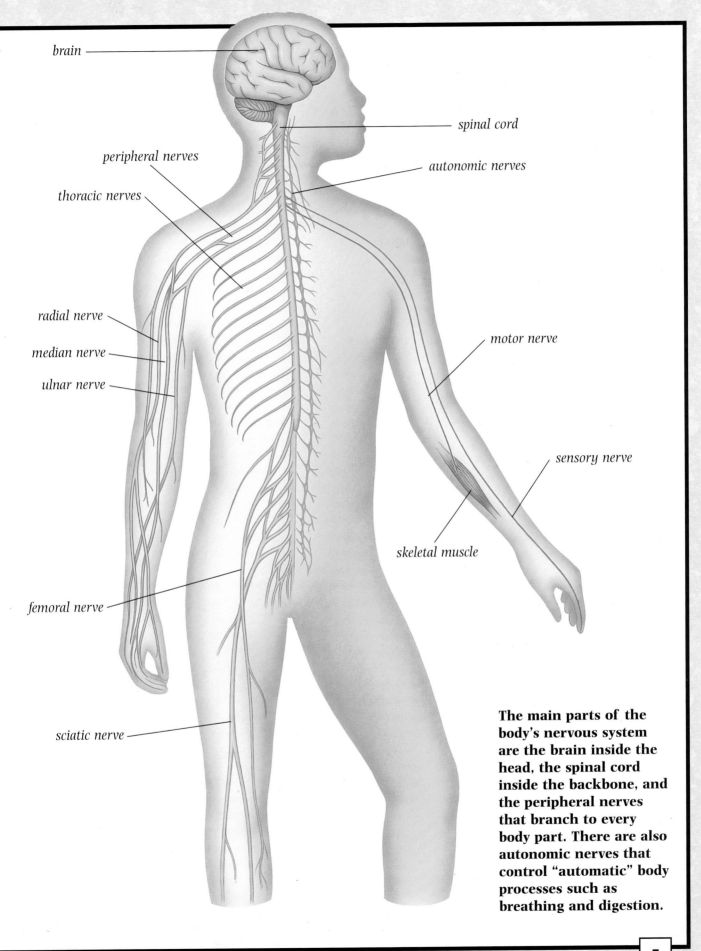

brain

spinal cord

peripheral nerves

autonomic nerves

thoracic nerves

radial nerve

motor nerve

median nerve

ulnar nerve

sensory nerve

skeletal muscle

femoral nerve

sciatic nerve

The main parts of the body's nervous system are the brain inside the head, the spinal cord inside the backbone, and the peripheral nerves that branch to every body part. There are also autonomic nerves that control "automatic" body processes such as breathing and digestion.

The Nerve Cell

The body is made up of billions of microscopic **cells** of many different shapes and sizes. Bone cells make bones, muscle cells form muscles, and liver cells make the liver. Nerve cells make the brain and nerves.

Nerve cells are also called **neurons**. The main part of the nerve cell, the cell body, is very similar to other cells, when seen under the microscope. It has tiny parts inside it, such as the **nucleus,** or control center, and the mitochondria to provide energy. But nerve cells are unusual cells, in that they have very specialized and complex shapes. Around the cell body are lots of long, thin, spidery-looking parts. These are called dendrites. There is also a longer, slightly thicker part, which is the axon, or nerve fiber.

The nerve cell's long, thin axon and dendrites resemble microscopic wires used to carry electrical signals inside computer circuits. In a way, they are. The brain and nerves work using tiny pulses of electricity, called nerve signals or impulses. These are passed among the billions of nerve cells in codes and patterns that represent information, like the bleeps of electronic codes inside a computer. The dendrites of a nerve cell receive **nerve signals** from other nerve cells. They pass them to the axon, which carries them a long distance, to the dendrites of other nerve cells in the system.

For nerve cells to pass nerve signals among themselves, they must be linked together. This happens at junctions called synapses.

The dendrites and axons do not actually touch in synapses. There is a tiny gap between them. But the nerve signal can jump the gap from one nerve cell to the next. It all happens incredibly fast, as billions of nerve signals flash around the brain and along the nerves every second. (The process of sending and receiving nerve signals through the massive network of nerve cells is explained on page 32.)

The nerve cell's axons and dendrites are so thin and fine that, for many years, they could not be seen even with the most powerful microscope. However, in 1873, the Italian neurologist (nervous system specialist) Camillo Golgi (1844–1926) discovered that a silver-containing stain, added to nerve cells, showed up their dendrites and axons clearly. This led to the discovery of synapses and many other important findings about the brain and nerves.

The brain and nerves are made of billions of nerve cells, or neurons. These have spidery-looking extensions. The smaller ones are dendrites, and the large one is the axon. These link together at junctions called synapses. Tiny pulses of electricity, known as nerve signals, pass through the network of nerves, carrying information around the brain and body.

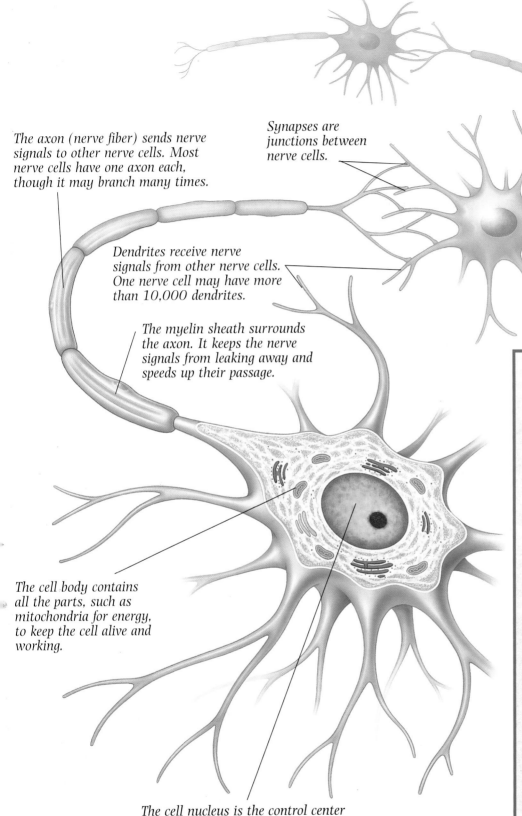

The axon (nerve fiber) sends nerve signals to other nerve cells. Most nerve cells have one axon each, though it may branch many times.

Synapses are junctions between nerve cells.

Dendrites receive nerve signals from other nerve cells. One nerve cell may have more than 10,000 dendrites.

The myelin sheath surrounds the axon. It keeps the nerve signals from leaking away and speeds up their passage.

The cell body contains all the parts, such as mitochondria for energy, to keep the cell alive and working.

The cell nucleus is the control center containing the genes, which tell the nerve cell how to grow and function.

FACT BOX

There are about 10 billion nerve cells in the brain and nerves.

The cell body of a typical nerve cell measures about 0.0008 inches (20 micrometers) wide.

The longest axons measure about 3 ft. (1 m), though they are microscopically thin.

If a typical nerve cell's body were enlarged to the size of a tennis ball, its dendrites could be 33 ft. (10 m) long, and its axon could be well over half a mile (1 km) long.

Brain and Spinal Cord

The brain takes up the top half of the inside of the head. It is well protected from knocks and bumps by the curved bones of the skull. The skull bones have holes in them, where nerves pass through to join the brain itself. The 12 pairs of nerves that join directly to the brain are called **cranial nerves**. They branch out mainly to the head, face, and neck. One cranial nerve, called the vagus, has long branches down into the chest and abdomen.

The biggest nerve that joins to the brain is the spinal cord. It is not really a distinct nerve; it is more an extension of the brain itself. The spinal cord passes through a large hole in the base of the skull and along a tunnel formed by the row of holes inside the backbone or spinal column. It is about as thick as a finger, and in an adult it is 18 in. (45 cm) long.

The spinal cord is the brain's main link with the rest of the body. From the cord, 31 pairs of spinal nerves branch outward, into the body. The spinal nerves divide into smaller branches and snake between the stomach, muscles, and bones. These nerves carry nerve signals between the brain and body.

The brain and nerves make up the body's nervous system. This can be divided into three main parts, according to the structure of the nerves and the jobs they do:
- the brain and spinal cord together are called the **central nervous system** (CNS) because they are in the center of the body and at the center of the control and coordination processes.
- the other nerves branching outward are the peripheral nervous system, or PNS, because they reach the periphery (outer parts) of the body.
- the nerves near the center of the body, controlling automatic processes, are a subdivision of the PNS. They are called the **autonomic nervous system**, or ANS.

Each main lump and bulge of the brain has its own name. The brain gets narrower at its base, the medulla, and merges into the top of the spinal cord. The main spinal cord finishes about the level of the waist. The lowest part of the backbone contains individual nerves and fiberlike strands that fill the "tunnel" inside the backbone. ▶

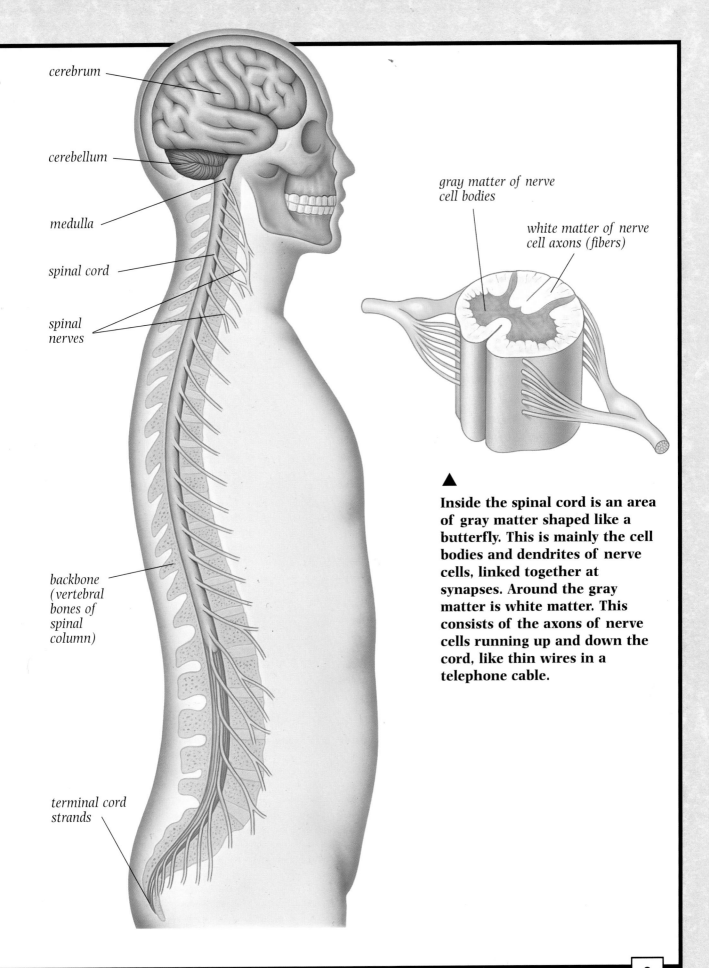

cerebrum

cerebellum

medulla

spinal cord

spinal nerves

backbone (vertebral bones of spinal column)

terminal cord strands

gray matter of nerve cell bodies

white matter of nerve cell axons (fibers)

▲

Inside the spinal cord is an area of gray matter shaped like a butterfly. This is mainly the cell bodies and dendrites of nerve cells, linked together at synapses. Around the gray matter is white matter. This consists of the axons of nerve cells running up and down the cord, like thin wires in a telephone cable.

Cranial Nerves

The 12 pairs of nerves that branch straight from the brain are called the cranial nerves. They pass through holes in the cranium, which forms the upper part of the skull. The cranial nerves are part of the peripheral nervous system, and they have the same appearance and structure as a typical peripheral nerve, as shown on the next page. Inside, each nerve is a bundle of thousands of axons, or fibers, of nerve cells, carrying nerve signals. So whole nerves are bundles of **nerve fibers**.

All the nerve fibers in a nerve look similar, but they are divided into two main types. These are called **sensory nerve** fibers and **motor nerve** fibers. The brain receives information along sensory, or afferent, nerves from the body's senses and sends out instructions along motor, or efferent, nerves to the body's muscles.

The various parts of the nervous system are well protected. The brain is surrounded and protected by hard skull bones. It is also wrapped in three sheetlike layers or membranes called the meninges. In addition, there is a layer of special liquid, cerebrospinal fluid, between the inner and middle meninges. These membranes and fluid are like shock absorbers that cushion the brain from shaking and jarring. The spinal cord is surrounded by the bones of the spinal column, which prevent it from kinking or twisting. The meninges and cerebrospinal fluid (CSF) extend from around the brain, down around the spinal cord, to protect it from damage.

The cranial nerves are in pairs, one on each side of the body. ▶
Like the peripheral nerves, some cranial nerves contain only sensory nerve axons, or fibers, so they are sensory nerves taking signals to the brain. Others have only motor nerve axons, or fibers, so these are motor nerves, taking signals from the brain. Others are mixed, containing both sensory and motor nerve fibers.

Cranial nerve 2
(optic nerve)
A sensory nerve from the eye to the brain; it carries nerve signals about sight.

Cranial nerve 3
(oculomotor nerve)
A motor nerve from the brain to the muscles behind the eyeball that turn and swivel the eye. The nerve also carries signals to the iris and lens muscles in the eye.

Cranial nerve 4
(trochlear nerve)
A motor nerve that works with cranial nerve 3.

Cranial nerve 5
(trigeminal nerve)
A mixed nerve that carries sensory nerve signals about touch from the eyes, nose, mouth, and face to the brain, and motor nerve signals from the brain to the jaw muscles, for biting and chewing.

Cranial nerve 6
(abducens nerve)
A motor nerve that helps cranial nerve 3.

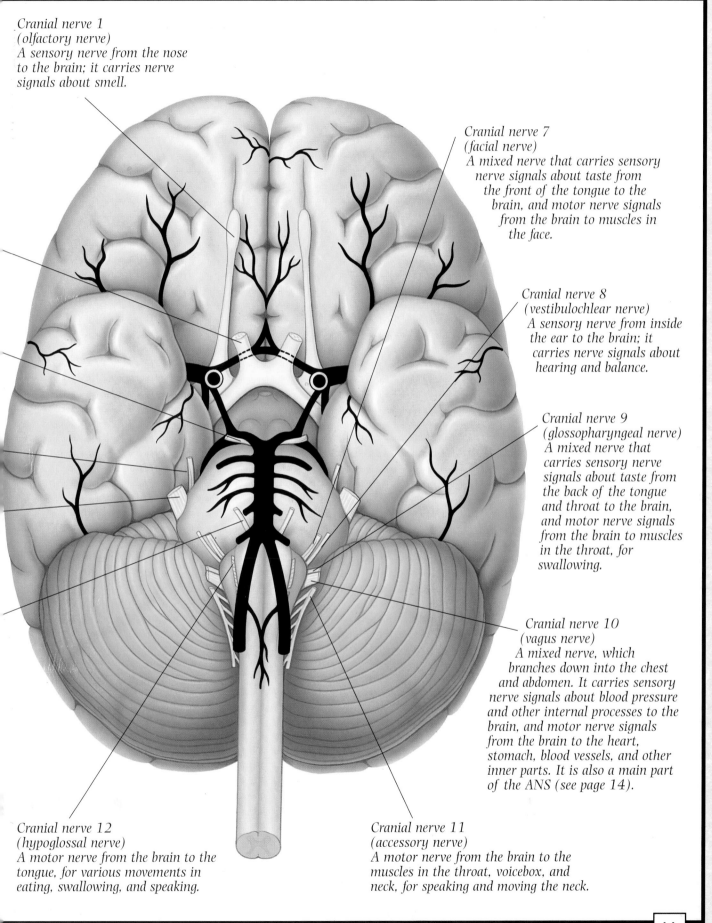

Cranial nerve 1
(olfactory nerve)
A sensory nerve from the nose
to the brain; it carries nerve
signals about smell.

Cranial nerve 7
(facial nerve)
A mixed nerve that carries sensory
nerve signals about taste from
the front of the tongue to the
brain, and motor nerve signals
from the brain to muscles in
the face.

Cranial nerve 8
(vestibulochlear nerve)
A sensory nerve from inside
the ear to the brain; it
carries nerve signals about
hearing and balance.

Cranial nerve 9
(glossopharyngeal nerve)
A mixed nerve that
carries sensory nerve
signals about taste from
the back of the tongue
and throat to the brain,
and motor nerve signals
from the brain to muscles
in the throat, for
swallowing.

Cranial nerve 10
(vagus nerve)
A mixed nerve, which
branches down into the chest
and abdomen. It carries sensory
nerve signals about blood pressure
and other internal processes to the
brain, and motor nerve signals
from the brain to the heart,
stomach, blood vessels, and other
inner parts. It is also a main part
of the ANS (see page 14).

Cranial nerve 12
(hypoglossal nerve)
A motor nerve from the brain to the
tongue, for various movements in
eating, swallowing, and speaking.

Cranial nerve 11
(accessory nerve)
A motor nerve from the brain to the
muscles in the throat, voicebox, and
neck, for speaking and moving the neck.

Peripheral Nerves

A computer receives information from many input devices, such as keyboards, cameras, microphones, and scanners. It also sends instructions to control many output devices, such as monitors, printers, speakers, and robots. All these various pieces of equipment are called peripherals and are linked to the computer by wires.

The brain and body work in a similar way. The brain is the center of the network. It receives information as nerve signals from the body's sense organs—mainly the eyes, ears, nose, tongue, and skin—and it sends instructions as nerve signals to more than 640 muscles all over the body. The brain is linked to all these body parts by the "wires" of the peripheral nervous system. Each nerve is a bundle of nerve axons, or fibers.

The largest **peripheral nerves**, such as the sciatic nerve in the lower hip, are as thick as your thumb. These branch until they become the thinnest peripheral nerves, finer than a hair and visible only under a microscope. In general, the thickest nerves contain the most nerve axons.

Sensory nerve fibers carry nerve signals from the sense organs to the spinal cord and brain. Motor nerve fibers carry nerve signals from the brain and spinal cord out to the muscles. Some peripheral nerves contain only sensory nerve fibers, so they are called sensory nerves. Others have just motor nerve fibers and are known as motor nerves. Others are mixed, with both sensory and motor nerve fibers.

The senses keep the brain informed about the surroundings by sending signals to it along sensory nerve fibers. Meanwhile, the brain makes the body respond and move about by sending out instructions along motor nerve fibers to the muscles.

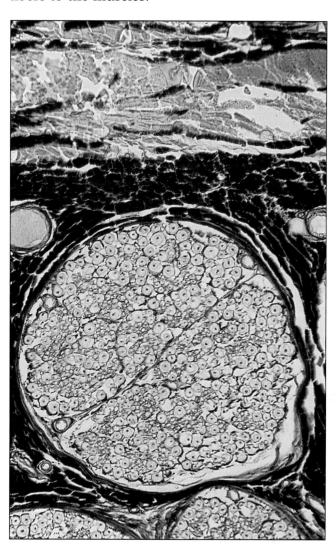

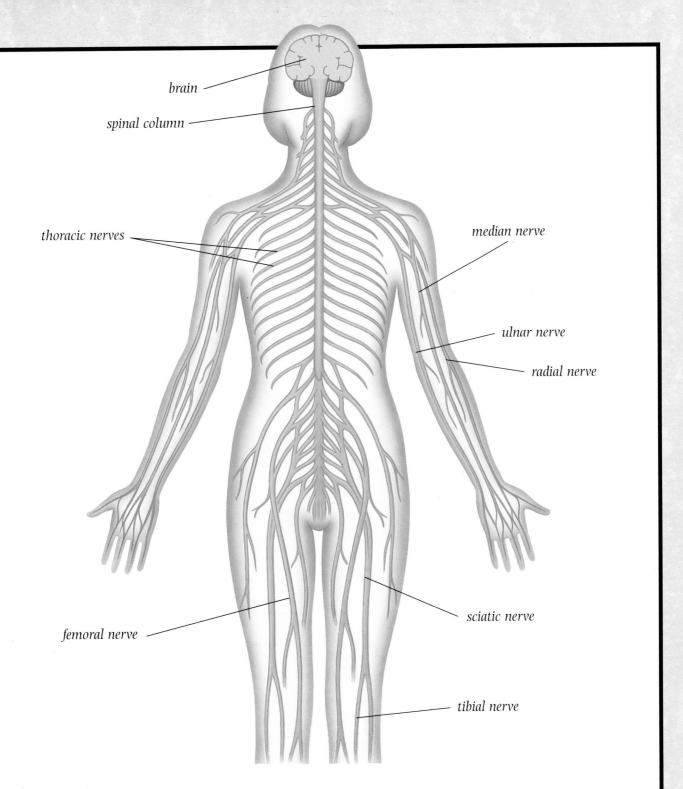

brain

spinal column

thoracic nerves

median nerve

ulnar nerve

radial nerve

sciatic nerve

femoral nerve

tibial nerve

◀ Each nerve is pale and flexible, like shiny string, and consists of small bundles called fascicles. These small bundles contain thousands of nerve cell axons carrying nerve signals (yellow, light brown, in the center of the picture). Some nerves have lumps or enlargements in them. These are ganglia, which are groups of nerve cell bodies and dendrites.

▲ Many of the peripheral nerves are named for the bones or muscles near them. The main nerves are the same in nearly every human body, but their tiny branches vary from one person to another. There are also plexuses, which are places where several nerves branch and come together and then separate again, exchanging nerve messages among them.

The Automatic System

The autonomic peripheral nervous system, usually called the ANS, is the body's "automatic" control system. It has parts inside the brain, spinal cord, and peripheral nerves, with connections to organs such as the heart and intestines. It shares some of the nerves of the peripheral nervous system, shown on the previous page. It also has its own nerves, nerve junctions, and links, which run mainly alongside the spinal cord, but outside the spinal column.

The ANS organizes and coordinates inner body processes that are essential to life, including
- the rate and strength of the heartbeat
- control of blood pressure, as blood presses on the inside of its main tubes or blood vessels
- the rate and depth of breathing by the lungs
- digestion of food
- waste removal from the body, such as urine removed by the kidneys
- control of the levels of nutrients and essential body salts, minerals, and chemicals, such as sugar for energy.

If you had to think about all these processes every minute of every day, you would have little time left for other things. Also you would not sleep, since these processes happen all through the day and night. So they are automatic. They work by themselves to a certain extent, under the control of the ANS—although the ANS is, in turn, under the control of the brain. However, this control comes from parts of the brain that do not have to do with consciousness, and usually you are not aware of it. The effect of the ANS is to ensure daily maintenance, repair, and smooth running of the whole body. It uses the same types of nerve signals as the rest of the brain and nervous system.

The ANS works alongside another of the body's main systems, the hormonal, or endocrine, system. This uses body chemicals called hormones, which circulate in the blood to control the activity of body parts. Together, the chemicals of the hormonal system and the tiny electrical signals of the nervous system ensure the body's day-to-day growth, maintenance, and repair.

Sometimes your body reacts at once, without your even thinking about it. If you step on a pin, you pull your foot away immediately. These automatic reactions that make the body move outwardly are different from the ANS, which works internally. They are called reflexes. Sensory nerve signals about the sharp pin come from the skin of the foot, up the nerve in the leg, to the spinal cord. A nerve connection in the cord sends motor nerve signals back out to the muscles of the leg, to pull the foot away. This reflex connection "short circuits" the brain. By the time your brain is aware of what's happened, your foot has already moved. Reflexes help the body to react quickly and to avoid danger, when the brain is concentrating on something else.

The ANS has nerve axons that ▶ branch from the brain and spinal cord to the various body parts and organs. It has two subdivisions: the parasympathetic and sympathetic nervous systems. The parasympathetic ANS acts as a brake, slowing down parts of the body to work normally, as when the body is resting and inactive. The sympathetic ANS acts as an accelerator, telling other parts of the body to work harder and faster, when the body is very active or under stress. Normally, the two work in a balanced way, according to the needs of the brain and body.

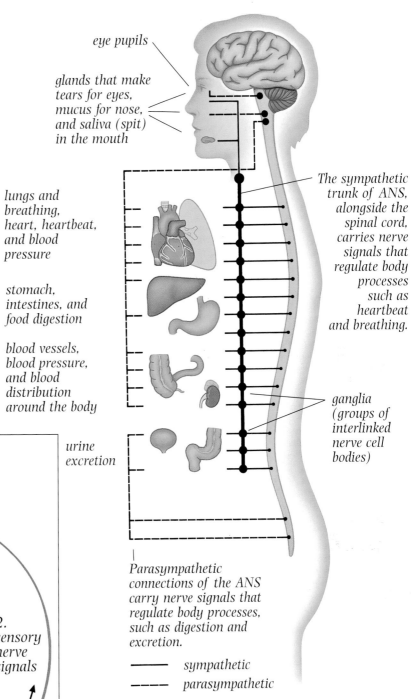

eye pupils

glands that make tears for eyes, mucus for nose, and saliva (spit) in the mouth

lungs and breathing, heart, heartbeat, and blood pressure

stomach, intestines, and food digestion

blood vessels, blood pressure, and blood distribution around the body

urine excretion

The sympathetic trunk of ANS, alongside the spinal cord, carries nerve signals that regulate body processes such as heartbeat and breathing.

ganglia (groups of interlinked nerve cell bodies)

Parasympathetic connections of the ANS carry nerve signals that regulate body processes, such as digestion and excretion.

——— sympathetic
- - - - parasympathetic

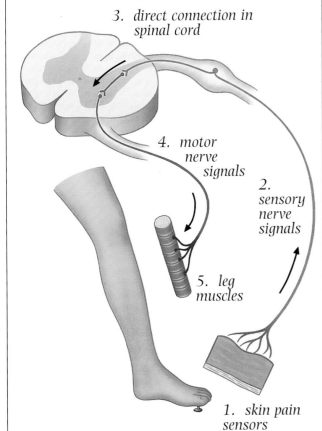

3. direct connection in spinal cord

4. motor nerve signals

2. sensory nerve signals

5. leg muscles

1. skin pain sensors

◀ A reflex is a fast response that seems to happen automatically. Nerve signals from sensors take a route directly through the spinal cord back out to the muscles.

Sight

The body has many senses. They all send sensory nerve signals to the brain. However, many of these senses deal with what happens inside the body. They measure the temperature and the levels of chemicals inside the body. We are not usually aware of them as they work. We are usually more aware of the five main senses that tell us what's happening outside the body. These are sight, hearing, smell, taste, and touch.

Sight is the sense that feeds most information to the brain. About two-thirds of what the brain knows, learns, and remembers comes in through the eyes, as pictures, words, written facts, and other visual experiences.

Each sense is specialized to change energy from one form, such as light rays, into the energy of tiny electrical nerve signals. The eyes deal with the energy in light rays. Each eyeball is about one inch (25 mm) across and fits neatly into a bowl in the skull bone, called the eye socket. The eye does not carry out all of the processes of sight. Like a movie camera, it detects the patterns of light rays: colors, shapes, movements, dimness, and brightness. The eye makes patterns of nerve signals from the patterns of light rays and sends the nerve signals to the brain. The brain analyzes the signals, recognizes shapes, colors, and movements and understands what is being seen.

The **retina** of the eye is about the size and thickness of a postage stamp. It changes light rays to nerve signals. This happens in millions of microscopic cells, named rods and cones from their shapes. Each eye has about 125 million rods and 7 million cones. The rods see well in dim light, but they cannot detect colors. They are mainly around the sides of the retina. The cones see colors and fine details, but they only work in bright light. They are concentrated at the fovea (yellow spot) at the back of the retina.

FACT BOX

The eye focuses on faraway objects by relaxing the ring of muscles around the lens, which makes the lens get thinner.

The eye focuses on close objects by contracting the ring of muscles around the lens, which thickens the lens.

For faraway objects, the muscles that move the eyes make the eyes look almost parallel to each other, into the distance.

For close objects, the muscles that move the eyes swivel to make each eye look inward, toward the nose.

The brain receives information from the lens muscles and muscles that move the eyes. It compares the views seen from each eye and is then able to judge distance accurately. This is called binocular, or stereoscopic, vision.

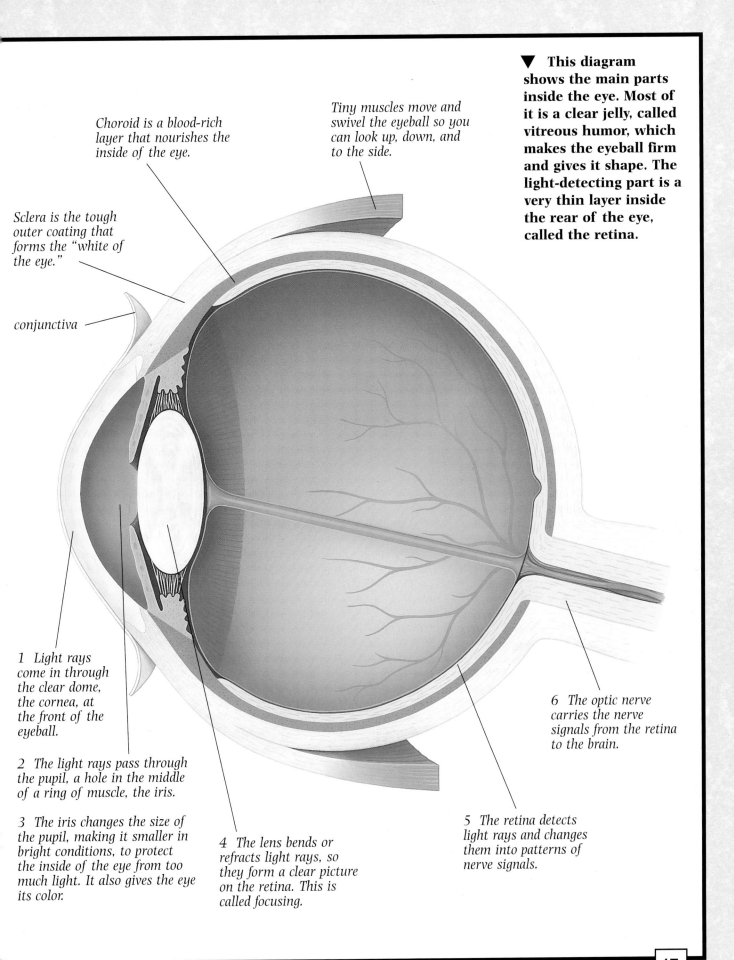

Choroid is a blood-rich layer that nourishes the inside of the eye.

Tiny muscles move and swivel the eyeball so you can look up, down, and to the side.

▼ This diagram shows the main parts inside the eye. Most of it is a clear jelly, called vitreous humor, which makes the eyeball firm and gives it shape. The light-detecting part is a very thin layer inside the rear of the eye, called the retina.

Sclera is the tough outer coating that forms the "white of the eye."

conjunctiva

1 Light rays come in through the clear dome, the cornea, at the front of the eyeball.

2 The light rays pass through the pupil, a hole in the middle of a ring of muscle, the iris.

3 The iris changes the size of the pupil, making it smaller in bright conditions, to protect the inside of the eye from too much light. It also gives the eye its color.

4 The lens bends or refracts light rays, so they form a clear picture on the retina. This is called focusing.

5 The retina detects light rays and changes them into patterns of nerve signals.

6 The optic nerve carries the nerve signals from the retina to the brain.

Hearing

Like the eyes, the ears are specialized to change energy from one form, into the energy of tiny electrical nerve signals. The form of energy that the ears detect is sound waves. These are invisible ripples or vibrations that travel through the air at about 620 mph (1,000 kph), fading as they go.

Sound waves travel quite slowly, especially compared with light rays. Sound waves coming from the side of the head reach the nearer ear a fraction of a second before reaching the other ear. Also, the ear on the far side hears slightly fainter sounds, partly because it is pointing away from the sound source. The brain detects the tiny differences in timing and loudness between the sounds in each ear. This is why, when you hear a sound, you can usually identify its general direction and look to see what made it.

The volume or loudness of a sound is measured in units called decibels (dB). The quietest sounds that a human ear can detect, such as a ticking watch, measure 10–20 dB. Everyday sounds, such as people talking and background music, are about 50–60 dB. Noises louder than 85–90 dB can damage the delicate hearing parts inside the ears. The longer the loud noises persist, the worse the damage. They can even lead to permanent loss of hearing.

Sound waves funnel into the ear canal and bounce off the eardrum. The sounds make the eardrum vibrate. The vibrations pass along a chain of three tiny linked bones—the hammer, anvil, and stirrup. These are named for their shapes, and they are connected at flexible joints. The vibrations pass on to the **cochlea**, deep in the ear.

The cochlea is filled with fluid and has a very thin, delicate, spiral sheet, or membrane, covered with tiny hairs growing from hair cells. Sound vibrations cause ripples in the fluid, which move and rock the membranes and tiny hairs, causing the hair cells to generate nerve signals. Different pitches or frequencies of sound, from deep low booms to high shrill hisses, vibrate different patches of hair cells.

The part of the ear that you can see on the ▶ side of the head is simply a "funnel" to help collect sound waves. The part that changes the sound vibrations into nerve signals is the cochlea, a structure shaped like a snail's shell. It is seated deep inside the head and is well protected by the skull bones.

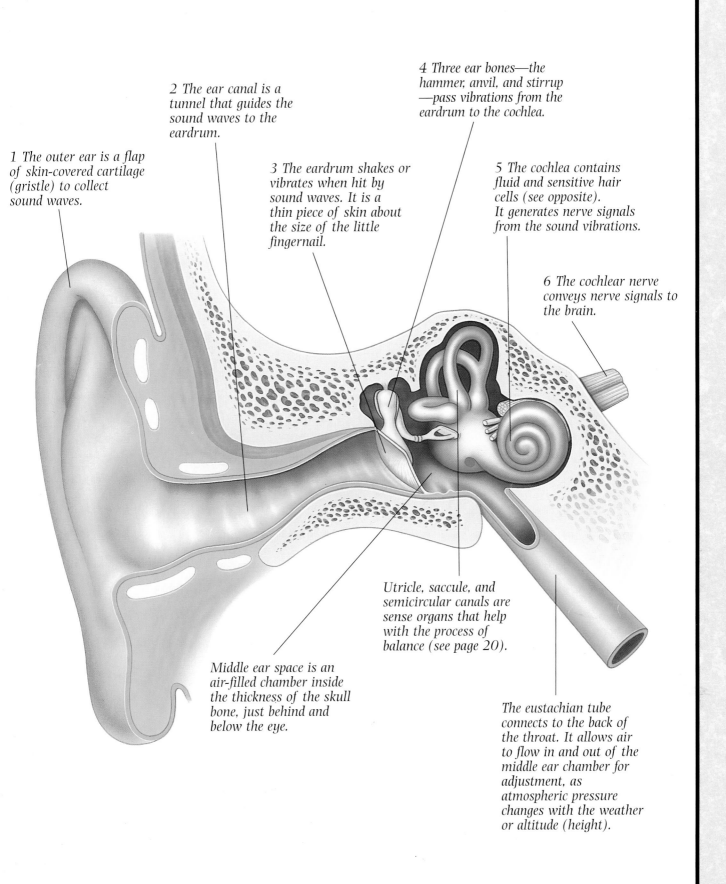

1 The outer ear is a flap of skin-covered cartilage (gristle) to collect sound waves.

2 The ear canal is a tunnel that guides the sound waves to the eardrum.

3 The eardrum shakes or vibrates when hit by sound waves. It is a thin piece of skin about the size of the little fingernail.

4 Three ear bones—the hammer, anvil, and stirrup—pass vibrations from the eardrum to the cochlea.

5 The cochlea contains fluid and sensitive hair cells (see opposite). It generates nerve signals from the sound vibrations.

6 The cochlear nerve conveys nerve signals to the brain.

Utricle, saccule, and semicircular canals are sense organs that help with the process of balance (see page 20).

Middle ear space is an air-filled chamber inside the thickness of the skull bone, just behind and below the eye.

The eustachian tube connects to the back of the throat. It allows air to flow in and out of the middle ear chamber for adjustment, as atmospheric pressure changes with the weather or altitude (height).

Touch, Smell, and Taste

Touch is detected by the skin. This sense is more complicated than it may seem. When you feel something, you not only detect its contact with your skin, but you also sense whether it is rough or smooth, hard or soft, wet or dry, sticky or slippery, or hot or cold. You can also feel if it is moving or vibrating and if it pricks or cuts you and causes pain. These sensations come from millions of microscopic sensors embedded in the skin. Some areas of skin such as the lips, eyelids, and fingertips have more microsensors packed more closely together. These areas are most sensitive to touch.

There are several types of microsensors in the skin, with thousands of each type all over the body. They respond to touch by sending a stream of nerve signals along their microscopic sensory nerve. These sensory nerves join together to form larger nerves, which carry the signals to the brain.

Each type of sensor detects certain features of touch, called stimuli. Some respond to the stimulus of very light contact, while others respond to heavy pressure or to heat and cold. However, each type of sensor responds to more than one kind of stimulus. It may react to several kinds, such as light touch, vibration, and warmth. The brain figures out the features of an object being touched by the very complicated overall pattern of nerve signals coming from all the stimulated sensors.

The body's fourth and fifth main senses are smell in the olfactory area of the nose, and taste in the taste buds on the tongue. As in sight, hearing, and touch, these sense organs feed nerve signals to the brain along sensory nerves.

Balance is a continuous process involving several senses as well as the brain and the muscles of the body. Some of the balance sensors are inside the ear. The three semicircular canals detect head movements in three directions: up-down, forward-backward, and left-right. The utricle and saccule detect other motions of the head and the downward pull of gravity. The skin detects pressure and weight due to gravity, especially on the soles of the feet. The eyes see what is upright and level in the outside world. The brain analyzes all the information from these senses and instructs the muscles to keep the body poised and well-balanced.

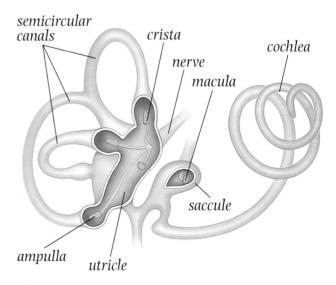

semicircular canals
crista
nerve
cochlea
macula
saccule
ampulla
utricle

▲ **This diagram shows the structures in the inner ear involved in balance.**

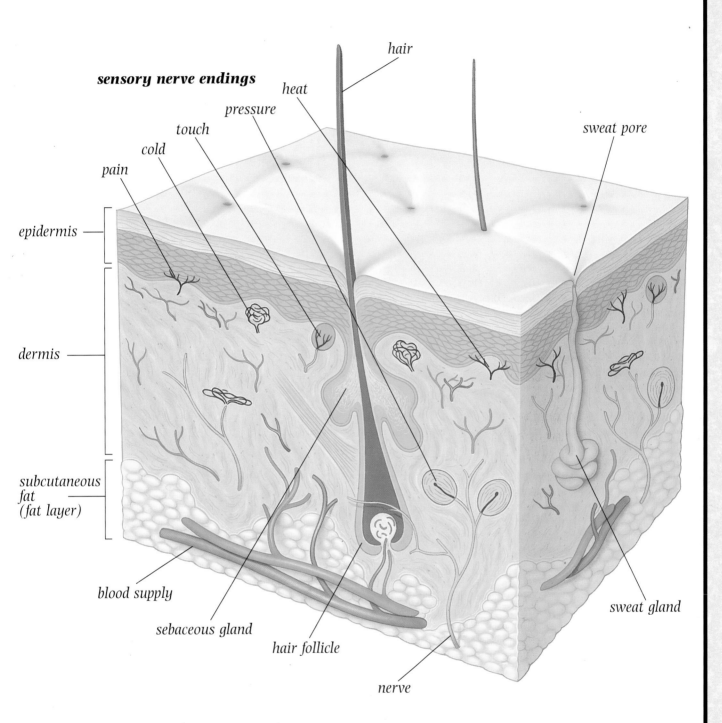

sensory nerve endings

hair

heat

pressure

touch

cold

pain

sweat pore

epidermis

dermis

subcutaneous
fat
(fat layer)

blood supply

sebaceous gland

hair follicle

nerve

sweat gland

▲ A typical piece of skin is about 0.04–0.08 in. (1–2 mm) thick. The upper layer, the dermis, consists of hard, tough, dead cells that give protection against rubbing and wear and tear. The touch microsensors are in the thicker, lower layer, called the epidermis. Most types of microsensors are named after the scientists who studied them under the microscope. Free nerve endings detect many stimuli, especially pain.

Inside the Brain

The brain has four main parts. These are the large, wrinkled halves of the **cerebrum** on top, the diencephalon below, the smaller wrinkled halves of the **cerebellum** to the rear, and the brain stem below and to the front.

The brain stem has three main parts. These are the midbrain, pons, and **medulla**. The lowest part, the medulla, merges into the spinal cord below. Inside these parts of the brain stem are many groups and lumps of nerve cell bodies and dendrites, called nuclei. Cranial nerve pairs 3 to 12 (see pages 10–11) join to the brain stem. It is also a junction for the millions of nerve fibers passing into it and through it, linking the spinal cord below, the cerebrum above, and the cerebellum to the rear.

The brain stem is mainly the "automatic" part of the brain. Its different parts control essential life processes such as breathing, heartbeat, digestion, and waste disposal. The parts of the brain stem work mainly through the autonomic nervous system. Other parts help to control reflex actions, sneezing, coughing, swallowing, and vomiting.

In the brain stem, mainly in the medulla, many nerve fibers cross from one side to the other. For example, the right upper part of the brain, the cerebral hemisphere, is linked down through the spinal cord to the left side of the body. So the main right brain receives sensory touch signals from the left side of the body and controls the muscles on the left side of the body. Similarly, the left upper part of the brain is linked to the right side of the body and controls its muscles.

FACT BOX

The average brain weighs about 3 lbs. (1,400 grams).

On average, men's brains are slightly larger than women's. But women's bodies are smaller than men's. So women tend to have relatively larger brains for their body size.

There is no link between brain size and general intelligence. Some very smart people have average-sized brains, while some large-brained people are not at all smart.

The brain stem is mostly hidden by the much larger cerebrum above. It is mainly a throughway and junction for nerves and is the site of control centers for automatic body processes. ▶

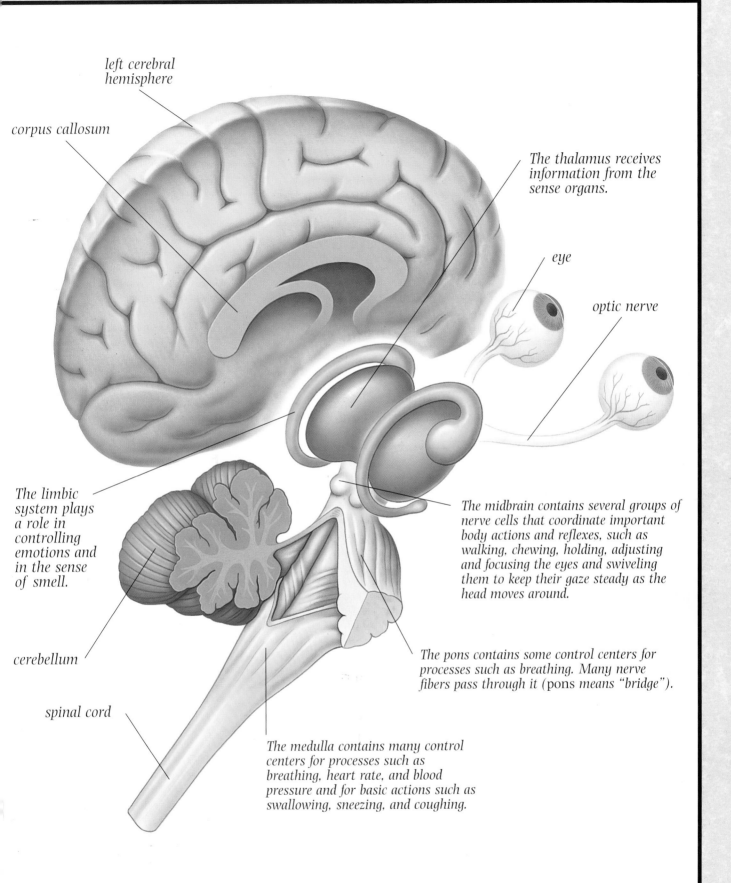

left cerebral
hemisphere

corpus callosum

The thalamus receives
information from the
sense organs.

eye

optic nerve

The limbic
system plays
a role in
controlling
emotions and
in the sense
of smell.

The midbrain contains several groups of
nerve cells that coordinate important
body actions and reflexes, such as
walking, chewing, holding, adjusting
and focusing the eyes and swiveling
them to keep their gaze steady as the
head moves around.

cerebellum

The pons contains some control centers for
processes such as breathing. Many nerve
fibers pass through it (pons means "bridge").

spinal cord

The medulla contains many control
centers for processes such as
breathing, heart rate, and blood
pressure and for basic actions such as
swallowing, sneezing, and coughing.

Movement

Have you learned a complicated activity such as playing the guitar, rollerblading, or gymnastics? At first, your movements are slow and awkward. But with practice, they gradually become faster and easier. With yet more practice you can carry out the actions almost without thinking.

When you were very young, you went through the same practicing process with basic movements such as standing, walking, and talking. Years later, they are so easy that you have probably forgotten how long they took to learn. Watching a young baby trying to walk or speak reminds people how difficult it was to learn these skills.

These types of precise, coordinated movements, from crawling and walking to playing musical instruments and sports, involve the cerebellum. It is the second-largest part of the brain, making up about one-tenth of the total weight. Its name means "little brain," and it looks like a smaller version of the brain's largest part, the cerebrum above it.

The cerebellum is linked by nerves to the spinal cord, and to the body muscles below, to the diencephalon, and to the "thinking" part of the brain above, the cerebrum. When the cerebrum decides to make the body move, it sends nerve signals from its motor center. These signals travel along nerves to the relevant muscles and to the cerebellum. The muscles begin the action, as instructed.

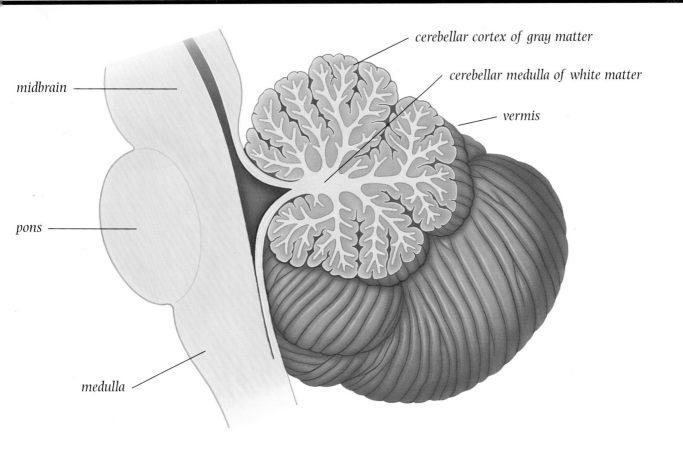

midbrain

pons

medulla

cerebellar cortex of gray matter

cerebellar medulla of white matter

vermis

The progress of the action is monitored by microscopic sensors, called proprioceptors, in the muscles, tendons, and joints all over the body. These detect changes caused by the shortening and stretching of muscles, the bending or straightening of joints, and the body's overall posture and balance. The proprioceptors send sensory signals back along nerves to the brain's cerebellum.

This type of return information is called feedback. The cerebellum compares the feedback from the body's proprioceptors to the original instructions for movement from the cerebrum. The cerebrum works out how the motion is progressing and detects any differences or problems and how to correct them. It feeds this

This boy is playing a sitar. When a person is learning to play a musical instrument, the brain must control dozens of muscles in the shoulders, arms, hands, and fingers.

▲ **The lobes of the cerebellum help to smooth and adjust the body's movements as these are learned and carried out.**

information to the motor center of the cerebrum so that the motor center can make adjustments as the body continues to move. This happens many times every second. The result is a smooth, precise, well-balanced action, which the cerebellum learns and then fine tunes.

Like the cerebrum, the lobes of the cerebellum have a gray outer layer called the cortex, made up of billions of nerve cell bodies. Inside are billions of nerve fibers, forming white matter, and groups of nerve cells called nuclei. The other main parts, the vermis and the flocculonodular nodes, help to control the muscles of the trunk and limbs so that the body stays upright and well balanced while it moves around.

The "Thinking" Brain

The main parts of the brain are the two halves of the cerebrum—the cerebral hemispheres. They are the "thinking" parts of the brain, the sites of our conscious awareness, thoughts, feelings, ideas, and memories.

Each cerebral hemisphere has three main parts. These are the outer layer or cerebral **cortex** of gray matter, the inner cerebral medulla of white matter, and the central curved lumps or lobes known together as basal ganglia.

The cerebral hemispheres' wrinkled appearance is due to the folding of their surface into bulges called gyri and grooves called sulci. Extra-deep grooves, called fissures, divide each hemisphere into main patches or lobes. These are named the prefrontal, frontal, parietal, temporal, and occipital lobes, mostly after the names of the curved skull bones around them.

The cortex is shiny, grayish pink in color, and about 0.16 in. (4 mm) thick. Its many folds and grooves give it a large total area. Spread out flat, the cortex is the size of an office desk. Its gray matter consists of 50 billion nerve cells, linked together by billions and trillions of dendrites. They form a huge network with many pathways and routes for nerve signals. Underneath the cortex, the white matter of the medulla is mainly the axons of these nerve cells, connecting them to the basal ganglia and other parts of the brain.

The two cerebral hemispheres are linked by a "bridge," the corpus callosum. This contains more than 200 million nerve fibers, known as commissural fibers. The corpus callosum carries nerve signals between the hemispheres, so that each half of the brain knows what the other half is doing.

Like a giant walnut, the wrinkled cerebrum is encased in the curved bones of the skull. Its outer gray layer, the cortex, is the site of conscious thoughts and feelings. It looks similar all over, but some parts of it are specialized to do certain jobs. For example, the basal ganglia are involved in memories and movements.

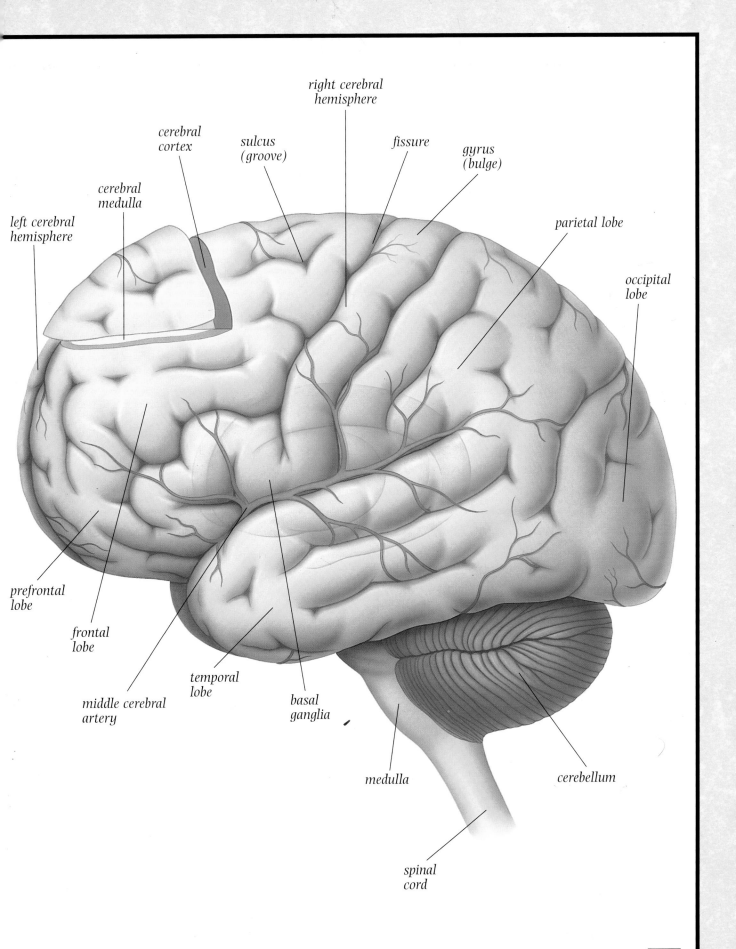

right cerebral
hemisphere

cerebral
cortex

sulcus
(groove)

fissure

gyrus
(bulge)

cerebral
medulla

parietal lobe

left cerebral
hemisphere

occipital
lobe

prefrontal
lobe

frontal
lobe

middle cerebral
artery

temporal
lobe

basal
ganglia

medulla

cerebellum

spinal
cord

Feelings and Urges

At the very center of the brain is its fourth major section, the diencephalon. It has two main parts—the thalamus, and below it, the hypothalamus. The thalamus consists of left and right parts, each about the size and shape of a small hen's egg. The parts have many nerve fibers going to the cerebral cortex and basal ganglia of the cerebrum above, to the cerebellum behind, and to the brain stem and spinal cord below.

The thalamus is a major junction point and processing center for nerve signals. It is sometimes called the "gateway to the brain." Many sensory nerve signals pass through it and are sorted and altered on their way to the cerebral cortex. Many motor nerve signals go through the thalamus between the cerebral cortex, the cerebellum, and the brain stem on their way out to the muscles.

Nerve signals connected with the overall level of brain activity go from the thalamus and the reticular system of the brain stem to other brain parts, especially the cerebral cortex and hypothalamus. These change a person's levels of awareness, from deeply unconscious to normal sleeping, dozing, resting, and wakeful, to fully alert. The thalamus, along with the limbic lobe of the cerebral cortex, is also involved in emotions and deep feelings such as anger, fear, terror, joy, and pleasure.

The hypothalamus is slightly larger than a red kidney bean, yet it has some of the most important roles in the entire brain. The hypothalamus is in overall control of vital body processes, such as breathing, heartbeat, and digestion, organized by the autonomic nervous system. It detects and adjusts the inner body temperature, to keep it normal. It causes you to feel thirsty and hungry when the body needs fluids and foods, and it tells you to stop drinking and eating when you've had enough. Along with the thalamus, the hypothalamus controls sleeping and waking and levels of alertness. It is the link between the upper parts of the brain and the autonomic nervous system. It makes the body react to strong emotions by actions such as screaming, going cold with fear, blushing, and crying with happiness or sadness.

The body has two major control systems. One is the brain and nerves. The other is the hormonal, or endocrine, system. Chemicals called hormones are made by glands around the body. These hormones circulate in the blood and affect the activity of cells and organs. The hypothalamus is the link between the two systems. Hanging on a stalk below the hypothalamus is the pituitary gland. This is the chief hormonal gland. It makes hormones and chemicals that control other hormone-making glands. In this way the pituitary and hypothalamus coordinate the nervous and hormonal systems. The nervous system usually works fast, within seconds and minutes, whereas the hormonal system usually works more slowly, over days, months, and years.

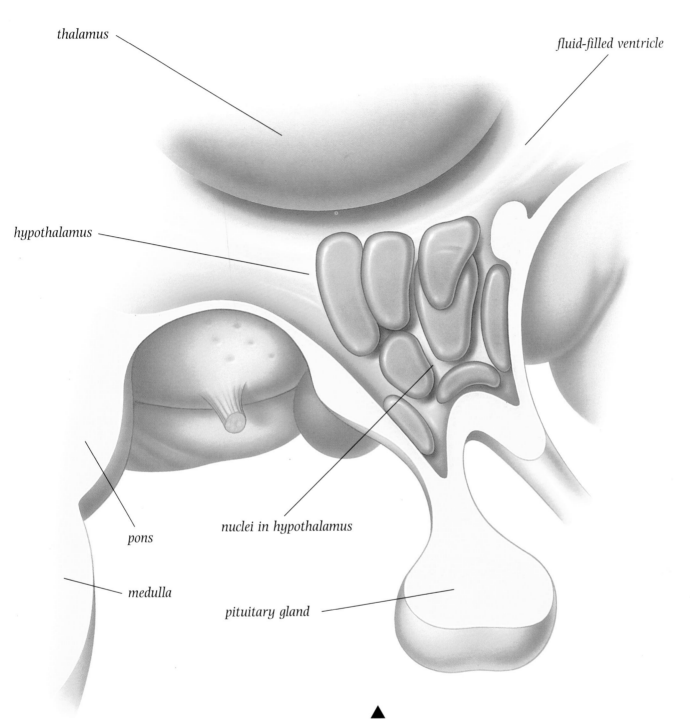

thalamus

fluid-filled ventricle

hypothalamus

pons

nuclei in hypothalamus

medulla

pituitary gland

▲

The thalamus is shaped like two eggs and lies at the lower front of the brain. The hypothalamus is a small lump of nerve cells just below it. Although very small, the hypothalamus is in charge of many of the body's most vital actions such as eating, drinking, and reproducing.

The Brain's Blood Supply

All parts of the body need a continuous supply of blood. This sticky red fluid brings nutrients, oxygen, and many other substances that are vital for life. The brain is no exception. It, too, needs a continuous flow of blood. The blood is pumped out by the heart into the main blood vessels, the arteries. Several pairs of arteries carry bright-red, oxygen-rich blood to the brain. The biggest are the internal carotid arteries, on the sides of the neck. The vertebral arteries that run alongside the backbone in the neck also carry blood to the brain.

When they reach the brain, these arteries branch and split many times and become much thinner. They spread over and into the brain, carrying life-giving blood to all its parts. The blood supplies oxygen, glucose for energy, nutrients, and other substances to the neurons and other brain cells. Blood also collects and carries away the cells' waste products, such as carbon dioxide.

The low-oxygen, reddish-blue "stale" blood flows out of the brain into large spaces called sinuses. The sinuses are between the middle and outer layers or meninges around the brain —the arachnoid and dura. This blood then flows slowly into two large veins, the internal jugular veins, one on either side of the neck. Gradually, the blood goes back to the heart.

The brain is not solid. It has a system of chambers inside, called ventricles. These are separate from the blood system. The ventricles are filled with a pale-yellow liquid called cerebrospinal fluid (CSF). There are four ventricles, linked by small channels. The CSF also bathes the outside of the brain, in the space between the middle and inner meninges— the arachnoid and pia. CSF flows very slowly through the ventricles within the brain, and through the subarachnoid space around the brain, helping to deliver nutrients and to carry away waste products.

Most of the brain's blood is brought by the internal carotid arteries and the vertebral arteries, one of each pair on each side of the neck. It is taken away after use by the internal jugular veins. CSF flows much more slowly through the ventricles within the brain and the subarachnoid space around it. ▶

FACT BOX

The brain makes up only about one-fiftieth of the body's total weight.

Yet the brain uses up nearly one-fifth of all the vital oxygen and high-energy glucose (blood sugar) carried around the body in the blood.

This means, for its size, the brain uses up ten times more glucose and oxygen than most other body parts.

The brain receives about 24 fl. oz. (700 milliliters) of blood each minute.

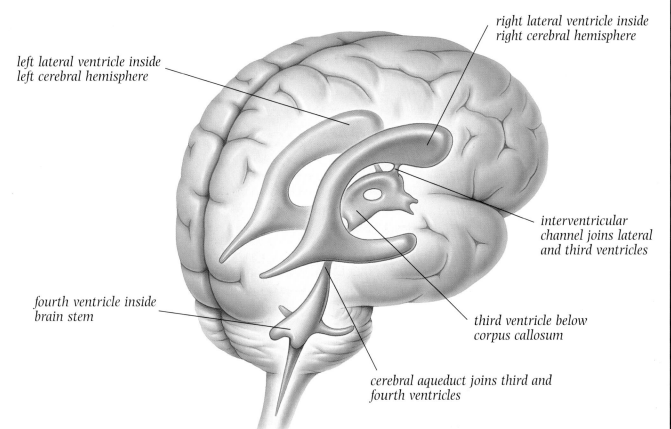

left lateral ventricle inside
left cerebral hemisphere

right lateral ventricle inside
right cerebral hemisphere

interventricular
channel joins lateral
and third ventricles

fourth ventricle inside
brain stem

third ventricle below
corpus callosum

cerebral aqueduct joins third and
fourth ventricles

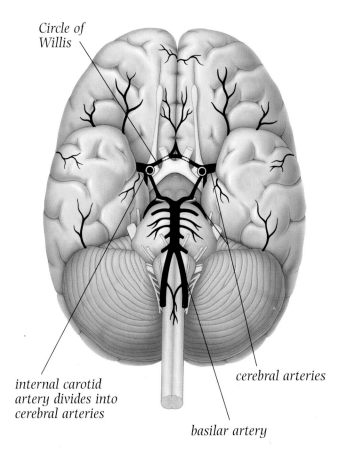

Circle of
Willis

internal carotid
artery divides into
cerebral arteries

cerebral arteries

basilar artery

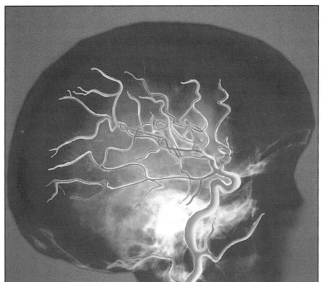

▲ Blood vessels and blood do not show up
on a normal X-ray photograph. But doctors
can inject a harmless dye that mixes with
blood and shows up white on an X ray. If
the dye is injected into the carotid artery, it
mixes into the blood going to the brain and
reveals the branching pattern of cerebral
blood vessels. This can be seen in the picture
above and is called a cerebral arteriogram.

The Nerve Impulse

Inside a computer, millions of tiny electrical pulses whizz around the electronic circuits. Their sequences and timing represent information such as words and pictures. These electric signals are the "language" of the computer system. The brain and nervous system are very similar. They also use tiny pulses of electricity as their language to represent information. The pulses are called nerve signals or, more accurately, **action potentials**.

Nerve signals come to the brain from the sense organs, such as the eyes and ears, carrying information about the outside world. Billions of signals arrive every second. Nerve signals also come to the brain from the body's inner sensors, which monitor blood pressure, temperature, and other internal conditions. Within the brain, these nerve signals are sorted, analyzed, and processed, generating yet more nerve signals. We are aware of some of this activity, as our thoughts, feelings, and memories. When we decide to do something, for example, reach for a book on a shelf, millions of nerve signals go from the brain out to the muscles to make them pull and contract.

Nerve cells, or neurons, are specialized to receive and send nerve signals. Each signal, or action potential, is like a tiny pulse or wave of electricity that passes along the neuron's outer skin, its cell membrane. The pulse is created by moving the chemicals sodium and potassium through the membrane, altering the electrical

balance. The result is a moving pulse of electricity along the axon. A neuron receives nerve signals from other neurons along its shorter, thinner dendrites. It sends nerve signals to other neurons along its longer, thicker axon. Every second, billions of neurons in the brain and nervous system receive and send billions of nerve signals.

FACT BOX

A typical nerve signal involves a change in electrical strength of about 100 millivolts, or one-tenth of one volt. This is 15 times weaker than a normal small flashlight battery of 1.5 volts.

On average, a nerve signal takes about 3 milliseconds (one three-hundredth of a second) to travel past any point on the neuron's cell membrane.

The covering of **myelin** around a nerve axon makes nerve signals travel faster. Nerve fibers with myelin sheaths carry signals at about 395 ft. per second.

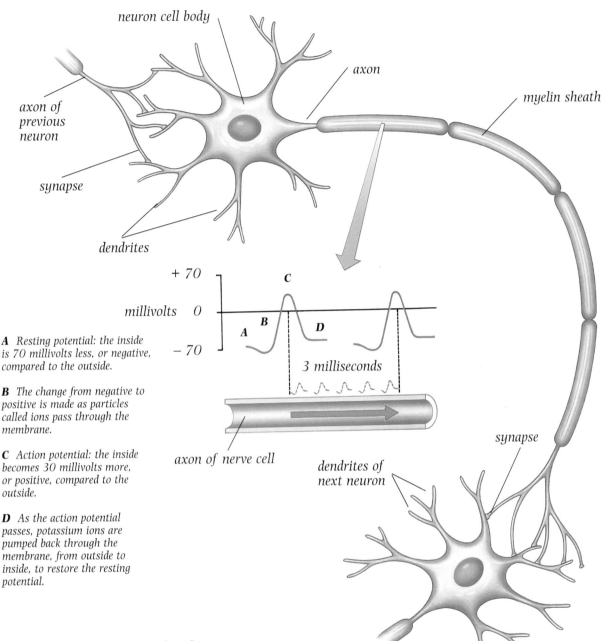

neuron cell body

axon

myelin sheath

axon of previous neuron

synapse

dendrites

+ 70

millivolts   0

− 70

C

B

A

D

3 milliseconds

A Resting potential: the inside is 70 millivolts less, or negative, compared to the outside.

B The change from negative to positive is made as particles called ions pass through the membrane.

C Action potential: the inside becomes 30 millivolts more, or positive, compared to the outside.

D As the action potential passes, potassium ions are pumped back through the membrane, from outside to inside, to restore the resting potential.

axon of nerve cell

dendrites of next neuron

synapse

Nerve cells link with each other at junctions called synapses. The two nerve cells do not quite touch at a synapse. There is a tiny gap between them, the **synaptic cleft**. The nerve signal arrives at the synapse as a wave of electricity, the action potential. This causes the release of chemicals called neurotransmitters. The chemicals seep across the gap to the next neuron, where they cause a new wave of electricity to begin. So a nerve signal changes from electrical form into chemical form to "jump the gap" in a synapse.

▲

A nerve signal is like a tiny traveling wave of electricity that passes along the cell membrane of a neuron. Normally the neuron is inactive, or resting. In electrical terms, its inside is slightly negative compared to its outside. When it sends a signal, the inside becomes positive compared to the outside, for just one-thousandth of a second. This traveling wave is called the action potential.

Brain Waves

The human body is a complex mixture of water, minerals, and salts. This means it is a good conductor of electricity, which is why it is dangerous to touch power lines or play with electric sockets. The millions of tiny electrical nerve signals whizzing around in the brain cause "electrical echoes" to pass outward in continual ripples. They travel through the brain's outer coverings (or meninges) and through the bones of the skull, to the skin of the scalp and head.

These tiny electrical ripples are too weak for us to feel. But they can be detected by metal sensors on the skin and fed into sensitive electronic equipment. There the signals are amplified or strengthened and displayed on a television screen or as wavy lines on a paper chart. The device that records these signals is called the electroencephalograph, or EEG machine. The resulting patterns of wavy lines are an electroencephalogram, or EEG trace.

In effect, the EEG shows electrical "brain waves." These change in size and shape according to whether the brain is thinking hard, daydreaming, resting, dozing, or going to sleep. EEGs can help doctors identify various brain conditions. These include epilepsy, brain tumor, stroke, and brain injury due to a blow on the head.

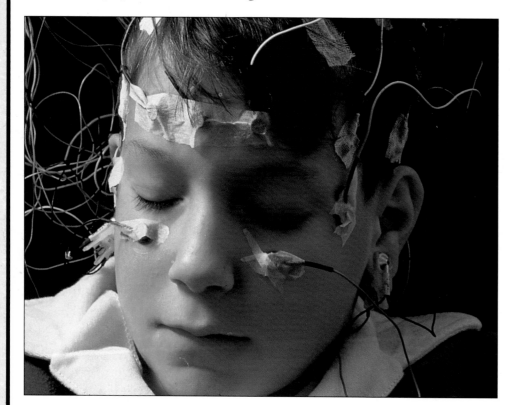

◀ **The EEG recording is painless and harmless. Physicians attach metal sensors called electrodes to areas on the skin of the scalp and head, using a special gel that easily wipes off later. The electrodes do not send electricity into the brain. They are recording electrodes, and they pick up the brain's natural electricity—its nerve signals.**

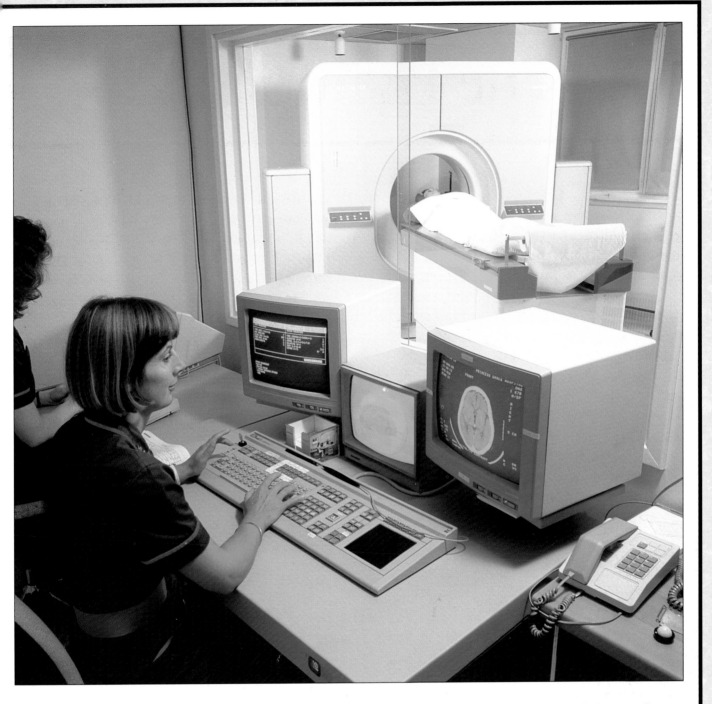

▲ The CT or CAT (Computerized Axial Tomography) scanner looks like a giant washing machine. It beams very weak X rays through the patient from many angles. A computer displays the results on a monitor.

There are now many ways of looking at the brain, by using different types of medical scanners. The CAT and MRI scanners reveal details of the brain's structure that do not show up on an ordinary head X ray. The PET scan shows which parts of the brain are most active and using up the most energy-giving glucose. These scans are painless and harmless. They are used to identify illness or other brain problems and for research into how the brain works.

The Brain Map

Our thoughts, feelings, emotions, and awareness happen in the brain, mainly in the gray, wrinkled outer layers, the cerebral cortex. The cerebral cortex consists of billions of nerve cells, linked by their dendrites to provide trillions and trillions of pathways for nerve signals. The nerve cells are joined to the inner parts of the brain by their axons. These form the inner "white matter" of each cerebral hemisphere, under the "gray matter" of the cortex.

The cortex looks much the same all over (see page 27), but patches of it are specialized for different jobs. These patches are called centers. There are different centers for different senses. For example, nerve signals from the eyes, representing what you see, pass along nerve fibers through the brain, to the visual cortex, or "sight centers." These are at the lower, rear part of the brain. Similarly, nerve signals from the skin go to the somato-sensory cortex, or "touch centers," which lie across the top and down the sides of the brain.

In most cases there are two centers, one on each side, on each cerebral hemisphere. However, most nerve fibers from one side of the body cross over in the upper spinal cord and lower brain stem and go to the other side of the brain. So each center deals with the opposite side of the body.

There is also a motor cortex, or "movement center," in each cerebral hemisphere. This controls the actions of muscles on the opposite side of the body. If a person suffers the condition known as a stroke and it affects mainly the right side of the brain, then the muscles on the left side of the body will be unable to work properly. The result can be paralysis of the left side of the body.

In the brain, nerve fibers carry smell signals. They have direct links with the cortex and with parts of the brain, such as the limbic system, concerned with deep-seated feelings and emotions. That is why a scent or aroma, such as a perfume or a musty house, can bring back powerful memories and cause strong feelings.

The nerve signals from the body's various ▶ sense organs are processed in different patches or centers of the cerebral cortex. These centers do not work in isolation. They constantly exchange signals among themselves. They also work with many inner parts of the brain, especially the thalamus, which helps process the nerve signals. Large parts of the cortex seem to have no specific job. These are called association areas. They are probably concerned with awareness, thoughts, feelings, decisions, memories, and other general mental processes.

Cerebral Cortex

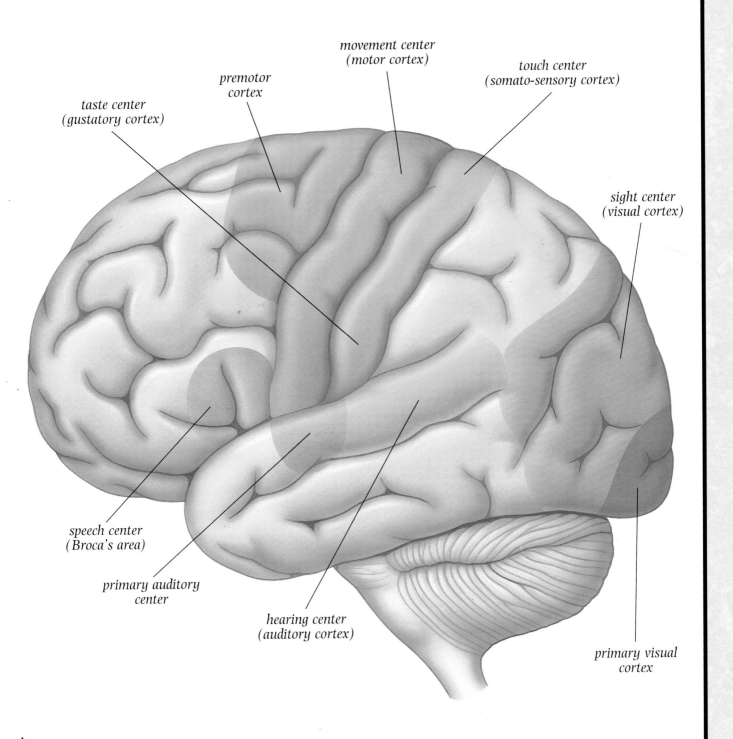

taste center
(gustatory cortex)

premotor
cortex

movement center
(motor cortex)

touch center
(somato-sensory cortex)

sight center
(visual cortex)

speech center
(Broca's area)

primary auditory
center

hearing center
(auditory cortex)

primary visual
cortex

The Two-sided Brain

The two sides of the brain, the cerebral hemispheres, look the same. They are both pinkish gray and wrinkled. But they do not work in the same way. Although both sides of the brain are involved in any task, the right side is more active, or dominant, for some tasks, while the left is dominant for others. The differences in the two sides of the brain develop gradually between the ages of about one and ten years.

In most people, the left cerebral hemisphere thinks about the parts that make up the whole. It takes charge in processes such as speaking, reading, and understanding words, writing, dealing with numbers and calculations, and working out problems in a logical, step-by-step fashion, as when carrying out a scientific experiment or working out the next move in a chess game. Since one side of the brain controls the other side of the body, the left hemisphere controls the right side, including the right hand, which most people use for writing.

The right cerebral hemisphere deals with whole things, without bothering too much about the parts. It takes charge in processes such as dealing with shapes from simple circles and cubes to faces and cars. It also deals with artistic and creative activities such as drawing, painting, sculpture, music, design, and with having ideas and insights. It tries to grasp and understand the whole picture and to recognize overall patterns and positions. It also controls the left side of the body, including the left hand.

▲

A much higher proportion of famous painters, sculptors, and musicians were left-handed compared with the proportion of left-handed people in the general population. This may show the effect of the more "creative" right side of the brain's controlling the left hand. Leonardo da Vinci, in the picture above, was a famous left-handed artist.

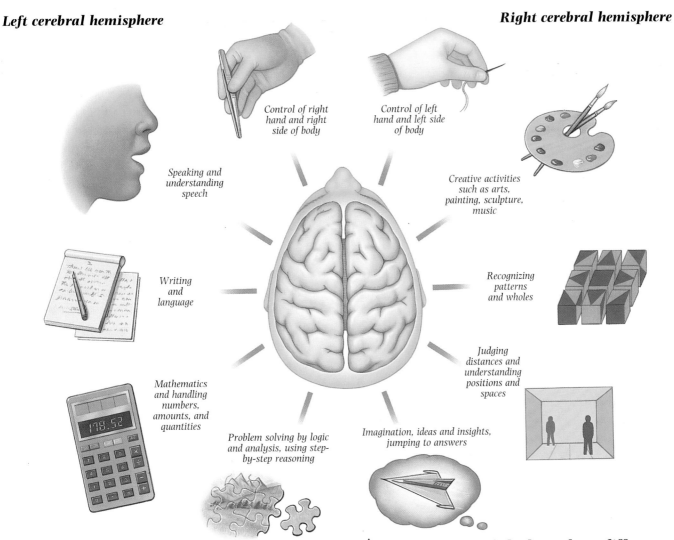

Control of right hand and right side of body

Control of left hand and left side of body

Speaking and understanding speech

Creative activities such as arts, painting, sculpture, music

Writing and language

Recognizing patterns and wholes

Mathematics and handling numbers, amounts, and quantities

Judging distances and understanding positions and spaces

Problem solving by logic and analysis, using step-by-step reasoning

Imagination, ideas and insights, jumping to answers

▲ **The two sides of the brain have different roles in thoughts and mental processes. The differences are not complete, since both sides are involved in all tasks. However, one side is dominant and takes the lead over the other.**

Speech is a special case. Usually, one hemisphere takes over the process of speaking. In most people, the speech center on the left side becomes dominant by about the age of eight. However, if the left side of the brain is damaged or diseased for some reason, the speech center in the right side develops and takes over.

Of course, the two sides of the brain work closely together. They exchange nerve signals along the corpus callosum between them, and they pass signals to and from the rest of the brain. In this way, the two-sided brain works as one complete control center.

About 11 people in every 100 are left-handed. This proportion is much the same all over the world, in different ethnic groups. A left-handed person uses the left hand for detailed tasks such as writing, sewing, and manipulating tools and utensils. The brains of left-handed people are not reversed. They are like the brains of right-handed people, as shown above, but the differences are less marked in left-handed than in right-handed people.

Thoughts and Memories

There is no single place in the brain where you think, remember, and learn. These processes are spread out among many brain parts, especially the "gray matter" of the cerebral cortex covering the cerebral hemispheres, as described on the previous pages. The cortex of the temporal lobes, on the front sides of the brain, is especially important for our awareness of what we are seeing, feeling, and doing, and the fact that we are alive, with thoughts and feelings—what is sometimes called consciousness.

A memory probably exists as a circuit or ▶ set of connections between nerve cells. The brain is continually making new sets of circuits as we learn and remember new things. This means making new synapses so that the nerve cells can pass signals along the circuit. Older circuits that are not used fade as their connections are lost. That is why we forget.

▼ The hippocampus, deep within the brain, helps to change short-term or fleeting memories into long-term ones that last for years.

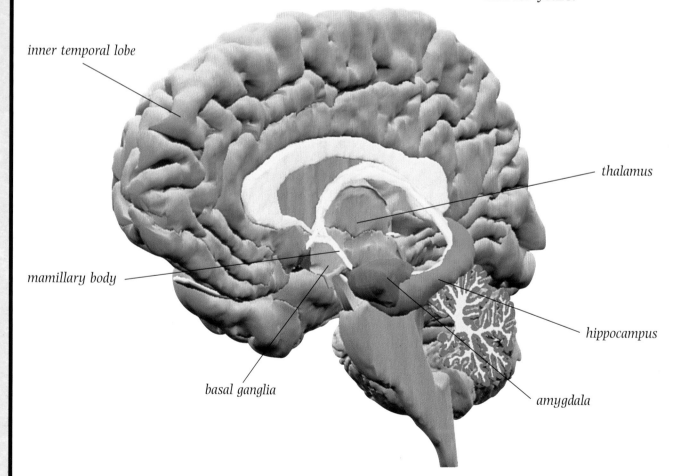

inner temporal lobe

mamillary body

basal ganglia

thalamus

hippocampus

amygdala

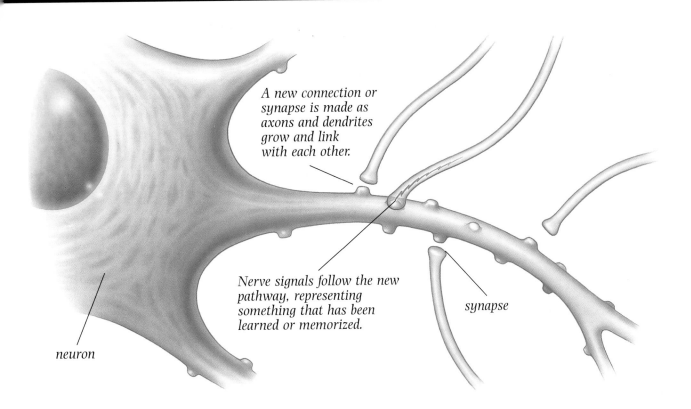

A new connection or synapse is made as axons and dendrites grow and link with each other.

Nerve signals follow the new pathway, representing something that has been learned or memorized.

synapse

neuron

We learn many things during our lives, and keep memories about them stored in our brains. They include

- body actions such as how to grasp, hold, crawl, walk, and talk, and physical skills such as riding a bicycle and playing a musical instrument
- mental skills such as reading, writing, counting, and arithmetic
- schoolwork and facts such as the names of presidents, how to spell words, and when the first astronauts landed on the moon
- how to behave, make friends, get along with people, and tell right from wrong.

What is a memory? It is probably a specific route or pathway that nerve signals can follow through the network of billions of nerve cells in the brain. This pathway is called a memory trace, and it seems that most memory traces are in the cerebral cortex. Since there are 50 billion nerve cells in the cortex, and each one can have connections with more than a thousand others, the number of

separate routes through this immense maze is truly astonishing.

There seem to be two main types of memory. One is short-term memory. We use it to store information, such as a telephone number or the score in a sports game, over a few seconds or minutes. Then it fades away. The other type is long-term memory, which stores information for months or years. Our names, addresses, birthdays, and similar important facts are in our long-term memory.

Many parts of the brain are involved in learning and memory. The hippocampus, deep inside the brain, seems to be involved in changing short-term memories into long-term ones over several days or a few weeks. If the hippocampus is damaged by injury or disease, the person still has old long-term memories and can make short-term ones. But he or she cannot change new short-term memories into long-term ones.

Brain Problems and Treatments

The brain, spinal cord, and nerves can be affected by many kinds of injury, damage, and disease. Sometimes these affect the senses, for example, causing numbness and tingling in the skin instead of the usual sense of touch. Other problems affect the brain's control of the muscles, leading to movements that are jerky, uncoordinated, or weak, or even to paralysis. Other conditions affect a person's behavior, causing problems such as mood changes and depression. In the past, people with behavioral changes or mental problems were called "crazy" and punished or locked away. Yet simply talking and sharing problems can relieve stress and anxiety. Also, modern drugs and surgery can help people with brain and nerve problems.

▼ Neurosurgery is extremely delicate and detailed. This surgeon is removing a brain growth or tumor. He looks through a microscope to see an enlarged view of the patient's head and brain (which are under the black cover). The same view is shown on the TV monitor behind.

Operations on the brain and nerves are called neurosurgery. A neurosurgeon can operate on tiny bundles of nerve cells using a binocular microscope to see them. Nerve cells can grow new attachments and links under certain conditions, but they cannot multiply to make more nerve cells to replace those that die. So recovery from a brain or nerve problem usually takes some time. The person must "relearn" many movements and skills. New pathways between surviving nerve cells have to be made to replace the links between the cells that have died.

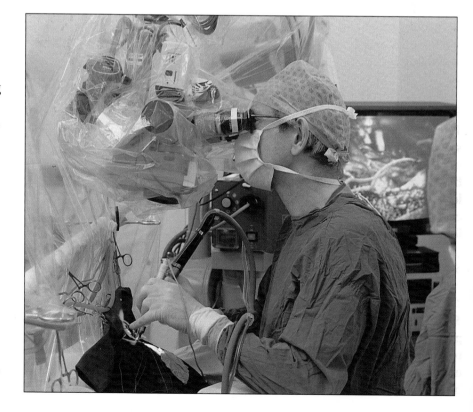

Alzheimer's disease

The brain shrinks as nerve cells die, and pieces of a protein called amyloid form in the brain tissue and disrupt nerve-cell connections. The cause is not known. The effects of the disease include loss of memory and understanding, changeable moods, and loss of muscle control.

Stroke

If a blood vessel to the brain or inside the brain becomes blocked, blood no longer reaches the nerve cells. They soon become damaged and begin to die. The result includes many and varied symptoms such as numbness, strange sights or visual disturbances, loss of muscle control, balance, and coordination, inability to speak, and paralysis. If one side of the brain is affected, the symptoms appear in the other side of the body.

Meningitis

In this condition, the meninges, or protective layers that cover the brain, are affected. They become swollen and inflamed, usually as a result of infection by germs. The symptoms include headache, nausea and vomiting, stiff neck, and sensitivity to bright lights.

Headache

This is not really a disease, but a symptom that accompanies many other conditions, from a bang on the head to lack of sleep. If headaches keep occurring, the doctor usually carries out examinations and tests to look for an underlying cause.

Schizophrenia

This is a mental illness that affects thinking, moods, and behavior. Sufferers become confused and perhaps afraid that people are trying to harm them and control their emotions. They may see visions and hear strange voices. Drugs used to treat this condition target certain areas in the brain such as the front cortex and limbic region.

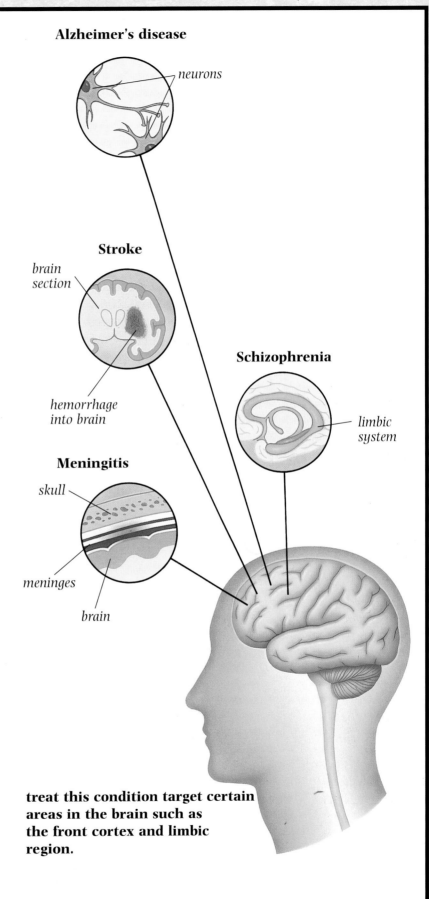

Alzheimer's disease

neurons

Stroke

brain section

hemorrhage into brain

Schizophrenia

limbic system

Meningitis

skull

meninges

brain

Sleep and Dreams

Each night the body rests and sleeps, relaxed and inactive. But the brain never stops. Its automatic control systems keep vital body processes, such as heartbeat and breathing, going. Recordings from EEG machines show that nerve signals continue to flash around the brain, but they are different than the patterns of signals when the brain is awake and alert.

Why do we sleep? During the night, the human body cannot do much, since it relies so greatly on sight to move around and to carry out tasks. So sleep may be an adaptation to the hours of darkness. The body rests to save energy. Its maintenance and repair processes mend the tiny amounts of wear, tear, and damage that occur

every day. The brain itself may carry out tasks such as sorting out the memories, thoughts, and feelings of the day before. All this time, the sleeping person is effectively unconscious. However, the senses still work for general survival. A strange noise or smell, such as smoke, causes a sleeping person to wake up.

Scientists can describe a typical night's sleep in terms of EEG "brainwaves" and the body's activities. There are four main stages of sleep. They occur in cycles lasting about one to one-and-a-half hours, gradually becoming "shallower" through the night. The REM stage means rapid eye movement. During this stage, a person's eyes move about and flicker back and

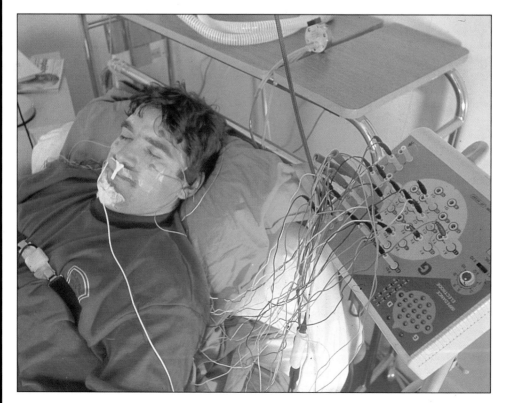

◀ **A man undergoing sleep tests. Electrodes record the brain's electrical signals and the activity of facial muscles. If someone misses the normal amount of REM sleep one night, he or she catches up by having extra REM sleep the next night.**

Many people, such as airport staff, work at night for several days or weeks. It can then take a few more days for the "body clock" to reset itself back to normal daytime activity. ▶

FACT BOX

The average amount of sleep needed usually decreases with increasing age. A newborn baby sleeps 18–20 hours each day.

A child of six needs about 10 hours each night.

A typical adult needs 7–8 hours of sleep each night.

Older people may sleep for only 6 hours and often nap for short periods during the day.

There is great variation in how much sleep people require. Some people feel well and healthy on three hours of sleep each night, while others need 12 hours.

forth, under closed eyelids. Dreams usually happen during REM sleep. Someone who is awakened during or just after REM sleep can remember the dreams. But if he or she is awakened some time later, the dreams are forgotten. This means that we all probably dream for many minutes each night, but we recall only the dreams we have just before we wake up.

However, no one really knows exactly what goes on in the sleeping brain, or exactly why we sleep. Yet it must be important. Lack of sleep, especially REM sleep, will kill a person more quickly than lack of food.

Scientists have recently discovered the basis of the body's built-in clock. This controls natural variations or biorhythms of physical activity, alertness, body temperature, digestion, urine production, hormone levels, and other body processes, over the 24-hour day-night period. The "body clock" consists of two lumps of a few thousand nerve cells each, called the supra-chiasmatic nuclei, in the lower front of the brain. These nerve cells are linked by other nerve cells to many parts of the brain and body.

Glossary

Action potentials Nerve signals—pulses of electrical energy that travel along the fibers, or axons, of nerve cells

Autonomic nervous system Nerves that control mainly "automatic" body processes, such as heartbeat and breathing

Axon See nerve fiber

Cells Microscopic living units—the "building blocks" of the body. There are billions of different types of cells.

Central nervous system The brain and spinal cord

Cochlea A structure found deep inside the ear that changes sound vibrations into nerve signals

Cranial nerves Peripheral nerves that join directly to the brain, rather than linking to it via the spinal cord

Cerebellum The two small wrinkled lobes at the lower rear of the brain; they are involved in making movements smooth and coordinated.

Cerebrum The top part of the brain consisting of the two cerebral hemispheres

Cortex The outer layer of some organs in the body, such as the kidney; in particular, the outer layers of the cerebral hemispheres of the brain

Medulla The inner layer of some organs in the body, such as the kidney. It is also the lowest part of the brain (medulla oblongata), where the brain merges into the spinal cord.

Motor nerve A nerve that carries signals from the brain or spinal cord to the muscles, to tell them when to contract and to produce movements

Myelin A fatty substance that surrounds many nerve fibers in the body. Myelin helps to speed the passage of the nerve message.

Nerves Pale, stringlike parts inside the body, made up of bundles of thin nerve fibers (axons) that carry nerve signals

Nerve fiber The long, thin, wirelike part of a nerve cell (neuron), also called an axon, that conveys nerve signals

Nerve signals Tiny pulses of electricity that move along a nerve fiber, also called action potentials. The patterns and timings of nerve signals represent information.

Neurons Nerve cells, specialized in shape and function to receive and to send nerve signals

Nucleus In a living cell, the dark spot or control center containing the genes, which tells the cell how to grow and function

Peripheral nerves Nerves that spread to all parts of the body and are linked to the central nervous system (brain and spinal cord)

Retina A very thin layer that lines part of the rear of the eyeball. It changes light rays into nerve signals.

Sensory nerves Nerves that carry signals from a sensory part of the body such as the eye, ear, or skin, to the brain

Synapses Junctions where two nerve cells almost touch

Synaptic cleft The tiny gap in a synapse, separating the almost-touching parts of two nerve cells

Books to read

Bryan, Jenny. *Mind and Matter*. Bodyguard. Morristown, NJ: Silver Burdett Press, 1993.

Burnie, David. *The Concise Encyclopedia of the Human Body*. New York: Dorling Kindersley, 1995.

Catherall, Ed. *Exploring the Human Body*. Exploring Science. Austin, TX: Raintree Steck-Vaughn, 1992.

Edelson, Edward. *The Nervous System*. Healthy Body. New York: Chelsea House, 1989.

Index

Numbers in **bold** refer to illustrations